Baby Doctor's Guide To Anatomy and Physiology Science for Kids Series

Children's Anatomy & Physiology Books

BABY PROFESSOR

EDUCATION KIDS

The human body refers to the whole structure of a human being. Each human body part is useful.

Read on to know more and understand our body!

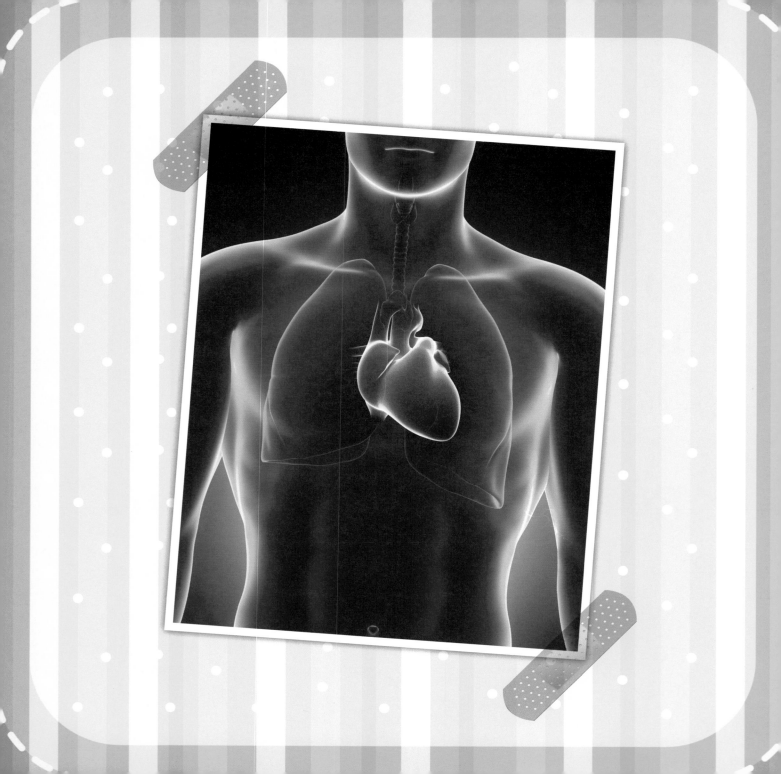

HEART

Body System: Cardiovascular System

Function: The heart pumps blood that provides oxygen and nutrients. The heart also assists in removing metabolic wastes.

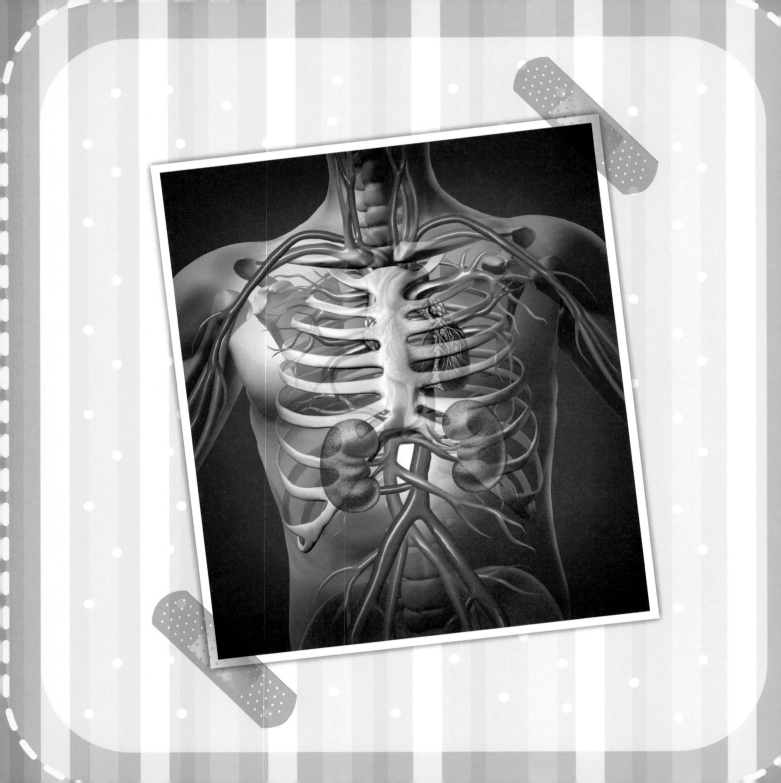

KIDNEYS

Body System: Urinary System

Function: They remove excess organic molecules and waste products of metabolism. The kidneys also serve as natural filter of the blood.

BRAIN

Body System: Nervous System

Function: The brain serves as the controller of the body. It is the source of "consciousness", which is the state of understanding what is around you.

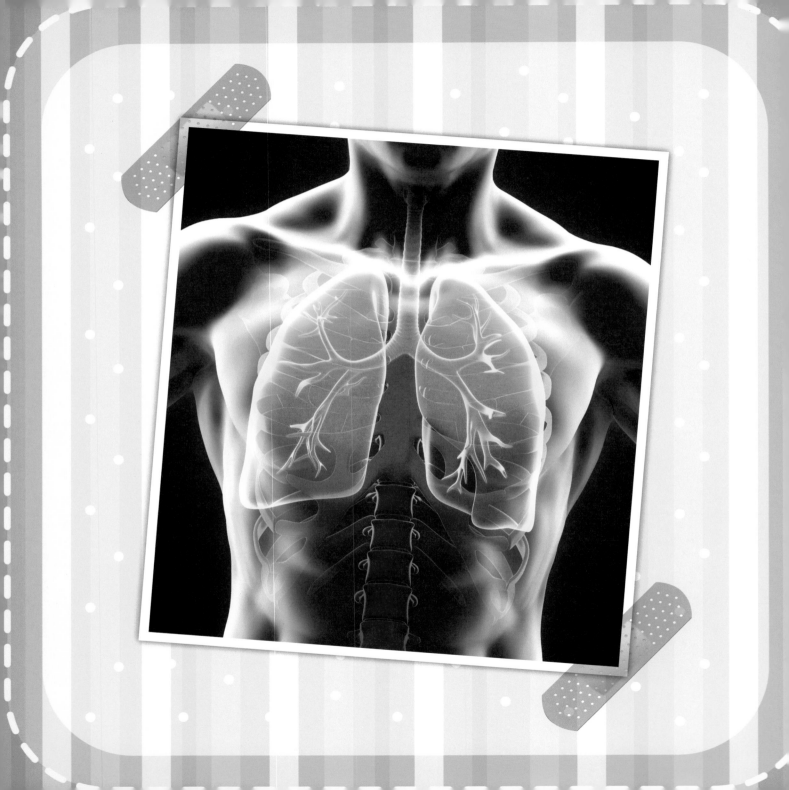

LUNGS

Body System: Respiratory System

Function: Its main purpose is to allow oxygen to enter the body, while removing carbon dioxide. Oxygen gives the body energy.

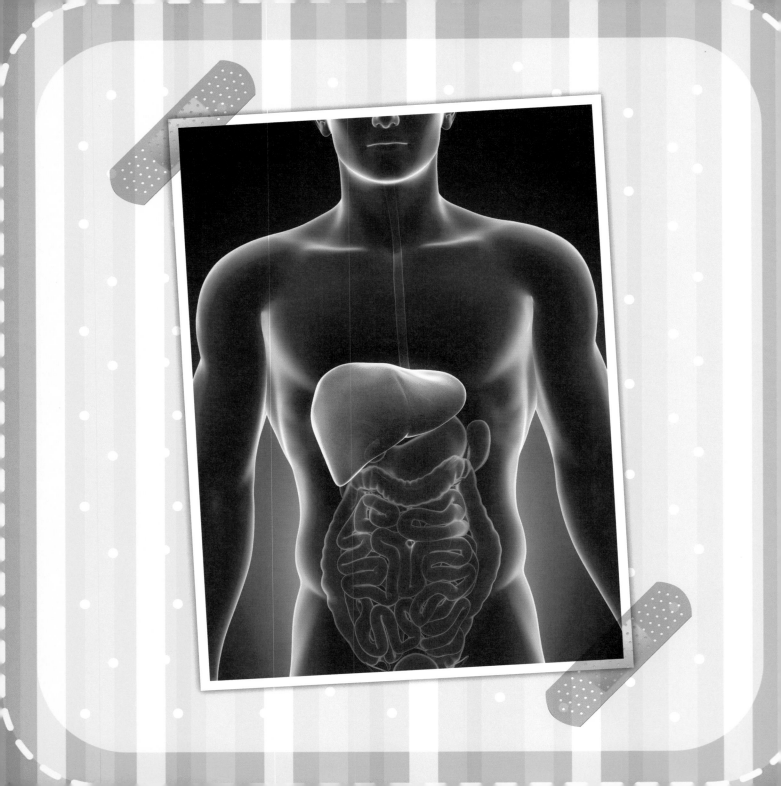

LIVER

Body System: Digestive System

Function: The liver detoxifies the blood to get rid of harmful substances. It also destroys old red blood cells.

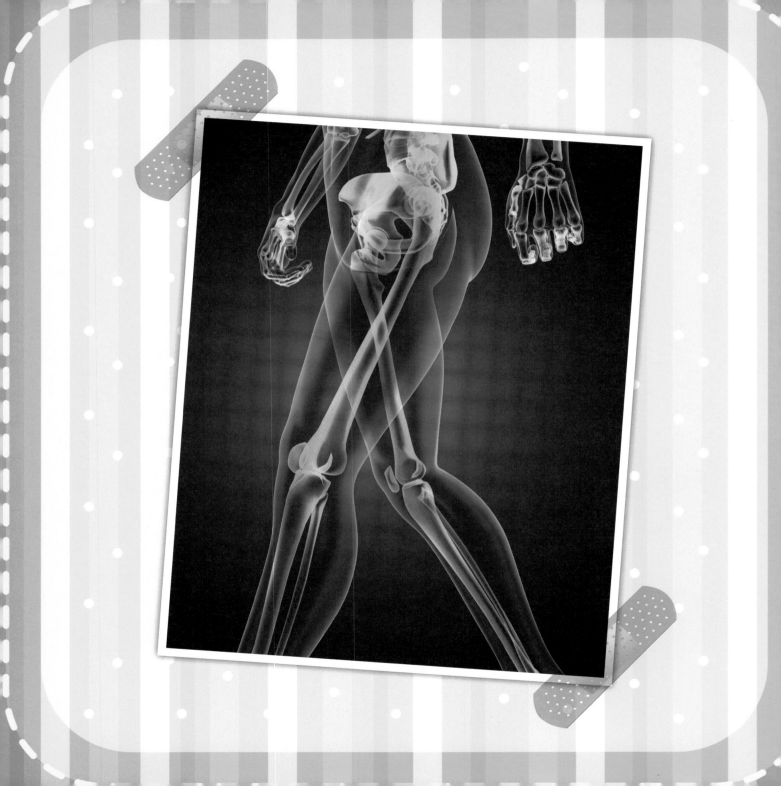

BONES

Body System: Skeletal System

Function: The skeleton is the framework of the body. A person cannot stand without bones.

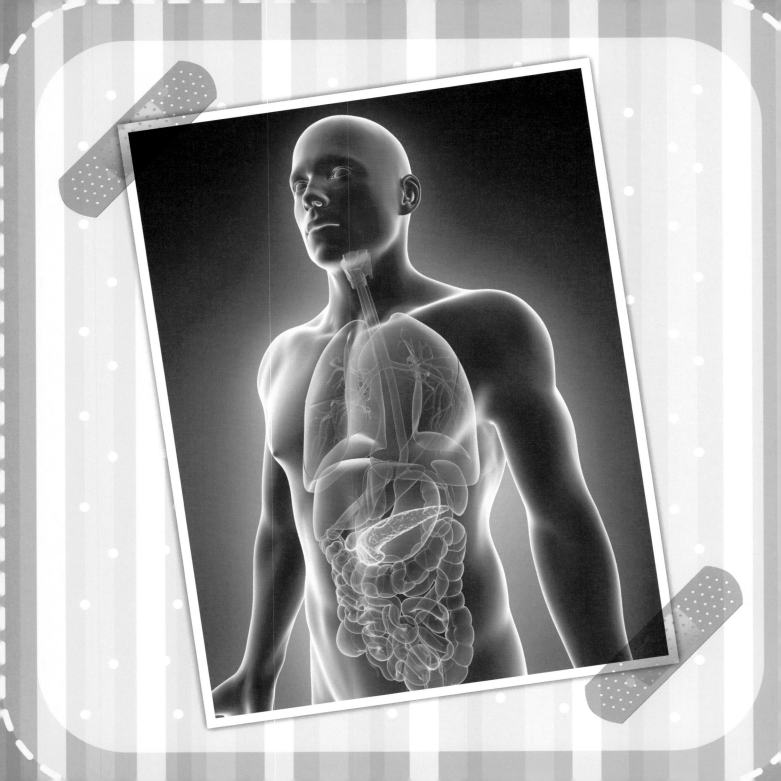

PANCREAS

Body System: Digestive System

Function: It secretes pancreatic juice that contains enzymes that helps with digestion.

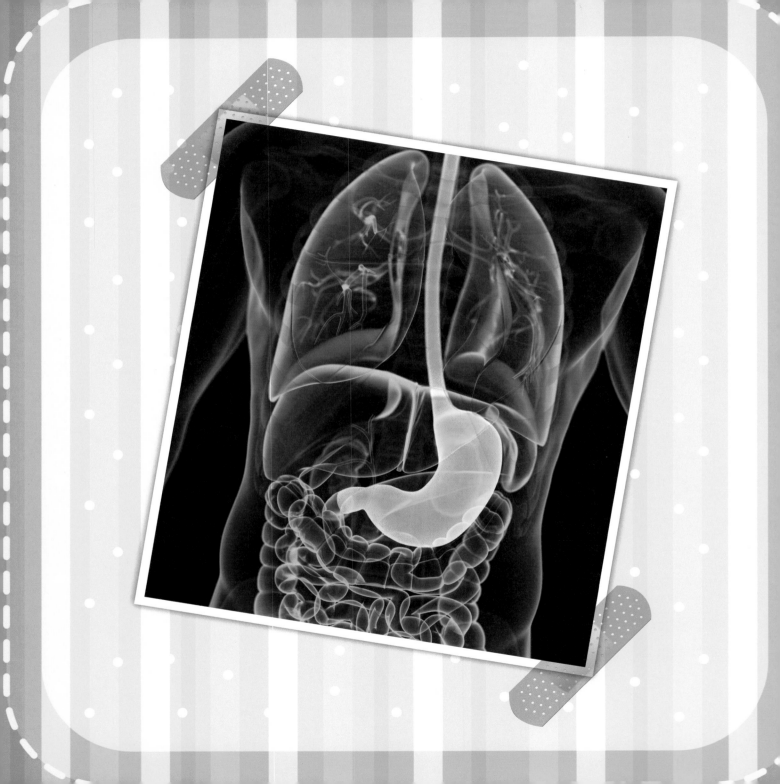

STOMACH

Body System: Digestive System

Function: Partial digestion takes place in the stomach. It is where food is temporarily stored.

GALL BLADDER

Body System: Digestive System

Function: This is where the fluid produced by the liver known as bile is stored before releasing it to the small intestine.

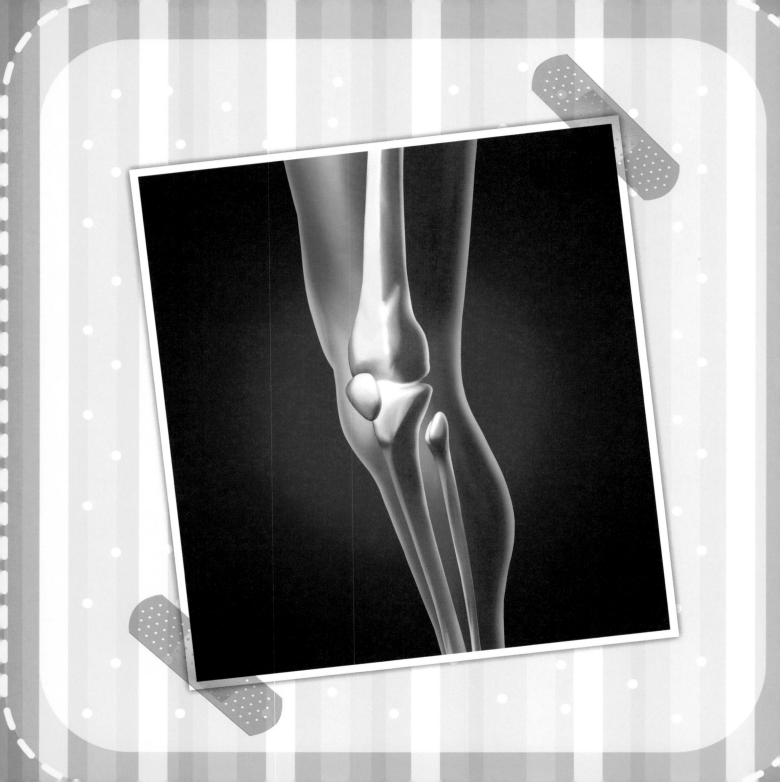

CARTILAGE

Body System: Skeletal System

Function: Cartilage is a gel-like filling between bones to protect joints. The cartilage helps maintain the shape of the area where it is present.

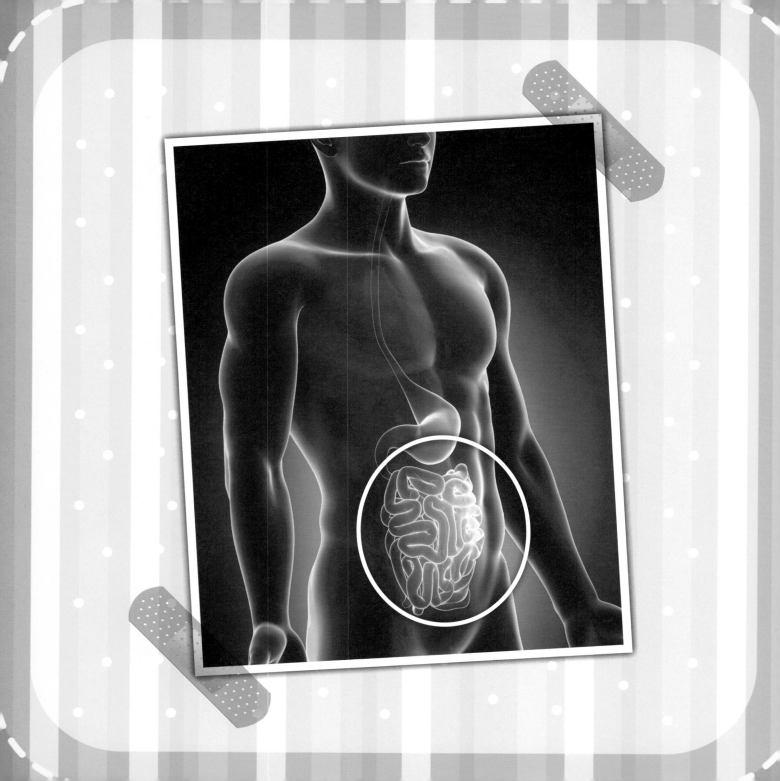

SMALL INTESTINE

Body System: Digestive System

Function: The small intestine is where the most chemical digestion takes place.

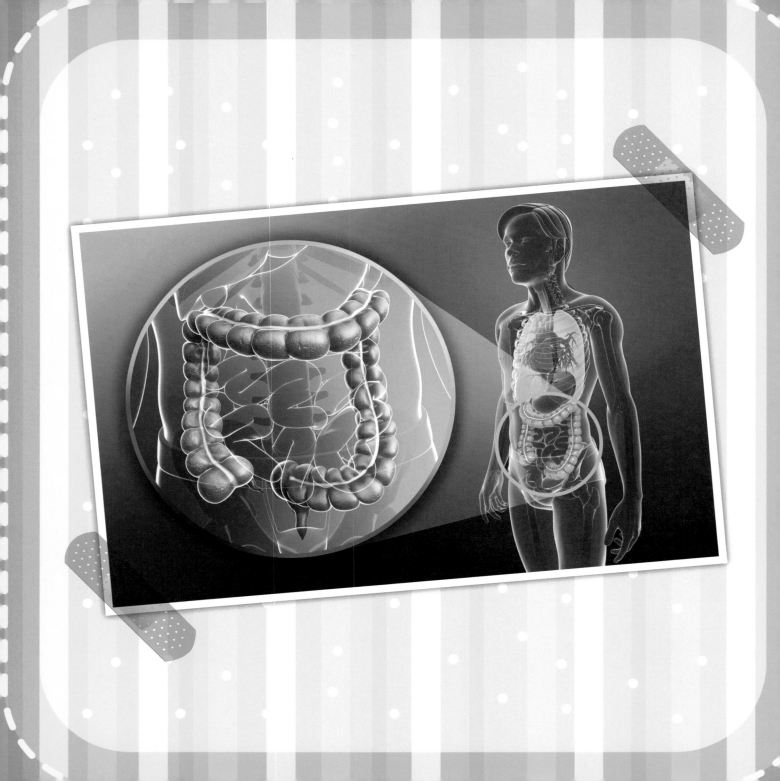

LARGE INTESTINE

Body System: Digestive System

Function: The large intestine removes water and other absorbable nutrients before moving wastes to the rectum.

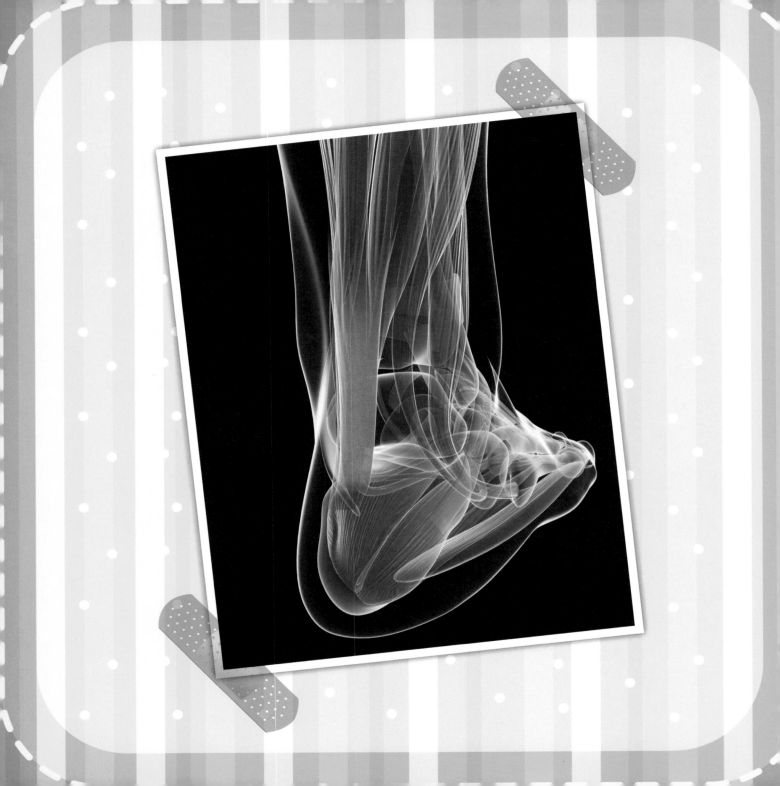

TENDONS

Body System: Muscular System

Function: Its main function is to connect muscle tissues to bones.

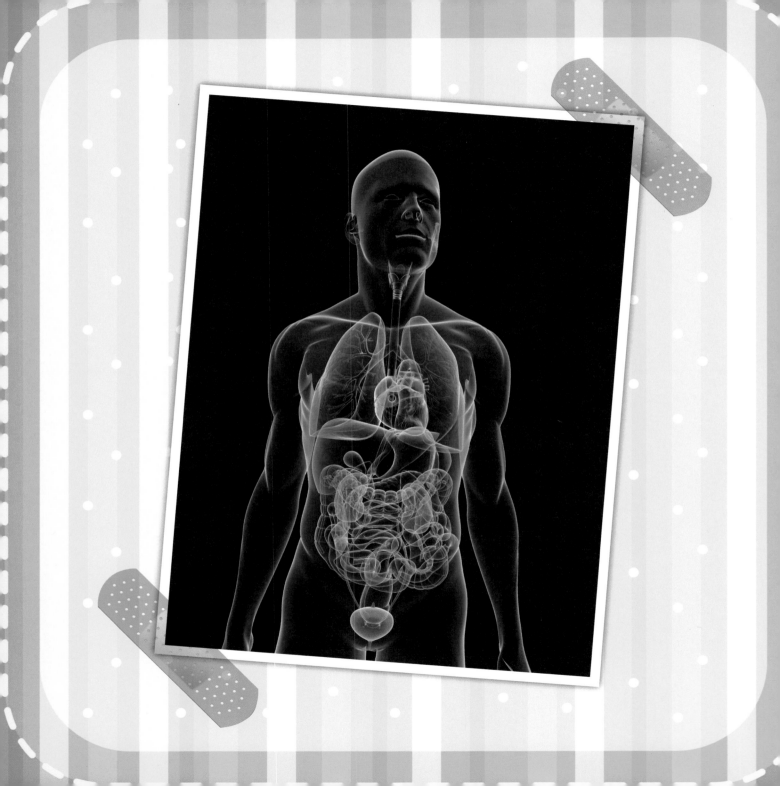

URINARY BLADDER

Body System: Urinary System

Function: Urinary bladder collects urine excreted by kidneys.

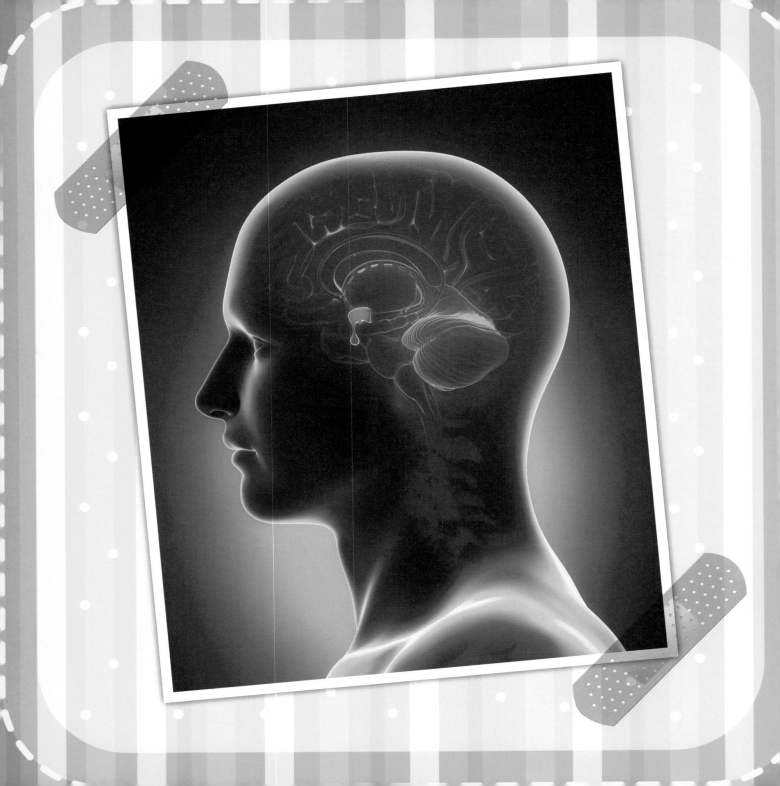

PITUITARY GLAND

Body System: Endocrine System

Function: Pituitary gland produces hormones that control many body functions.

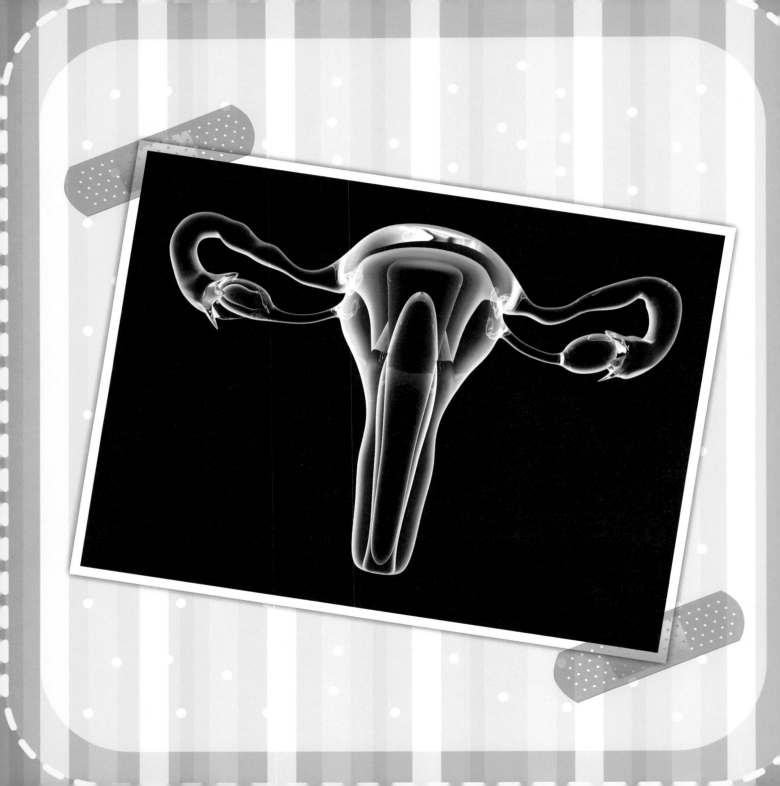

UTERUS

Body System: Reproductive System

Function: It is where babies develop and grow.

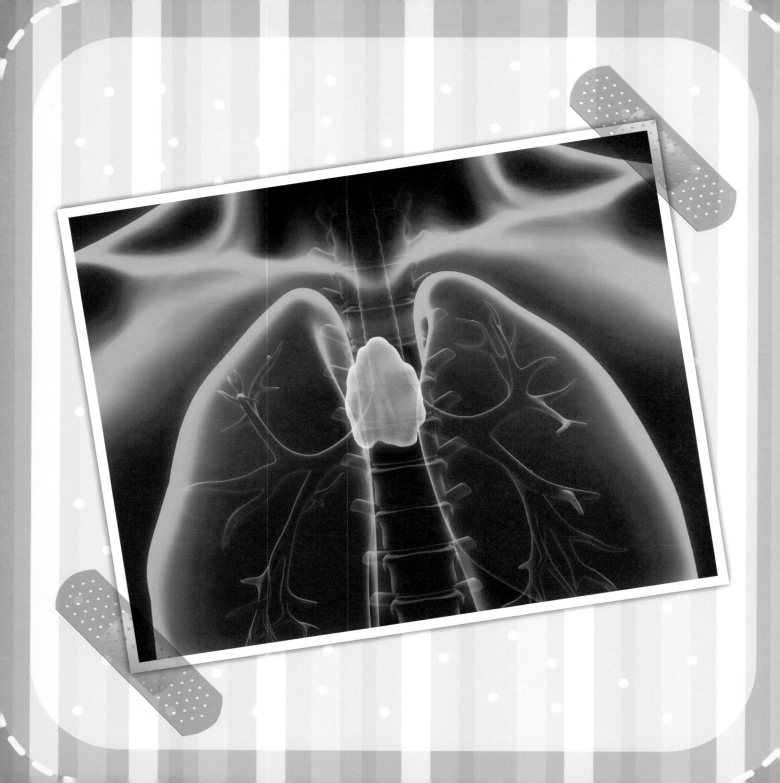

THYMUS

Body System: Lymphatic System

Function: The thymus helps develop T-lymphocytes that defend the body from deadly viruses.

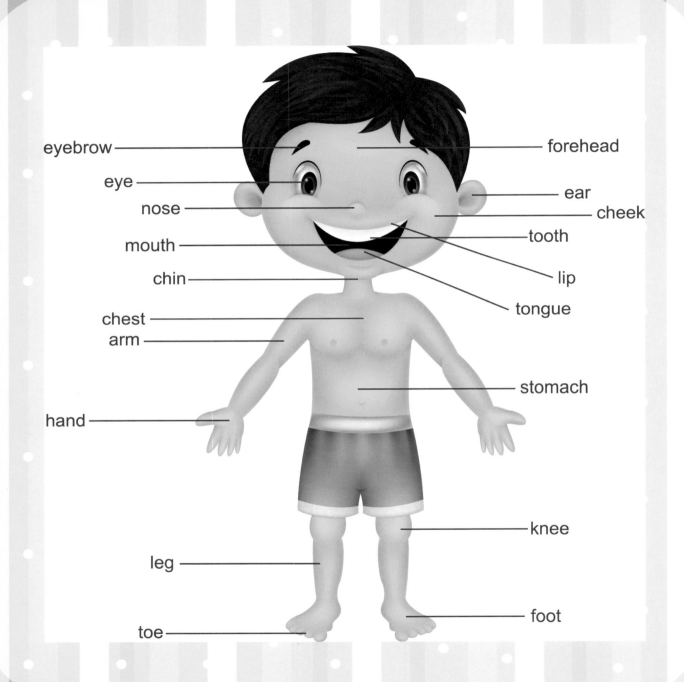

eyebrow

eye

nose

mouth

chin

chest

arm

hand

leg

toe

forehead

ear

cheek

tooth

lip

tongue

stomach

knee

foot

There are still many parts of your body. Research and learn more about your body!

Visit

BABY PROFESSOR
EDUCATION KIDS

www.BabyProfessorBooks.com

to download Free Baby Professor eBooks and view
our catalog of new and exciting Children's Books

Made in the USA
Columbia, SC
22 August 2024

40918434R00024